D1358267

Lee Canter

What To Do
When Your
Child Won't
BEHAVE

A Practical Guide for
Responsible, Caring Discipline

Lee Canter's Effective Parenting Books

Written by Patricia Sarka
Cover Illustration by Patty Briles
Design by Bob Winberry

Editorial Staff
Marlene Canter
Carol Provisor
Barbara Schadlow
Kathy Winberry

© 1994 Lee Canter & Associates
P.O.Box 2113, Santa Monica, CA 90407-2113
800-262-4347   310-395-3221

Printed in the United States of America
First printing May 1994

98 97 96 95 94 10 9 8 7 6 5 4 3 2 1

ISBN 0-939007-85-1

Raising a Well-Behaved Child

> I'm at my wits' end. I've tried everything to get my children to behave. I talk to them, I listen to them, I reason with them, and they still act up and talk back.

> My son is just too strong-willed for me to handle.

> I'm lost and overwhelmed because I really feel that I can't handle my kids.

Sound familiar?

Do you sometimes feel overwhelmed and powerless when dealing with your child's misbehavior? If so, you're not alone. Many parents feel that their children are more in control of their home than they are. And when parents feel continually frustrated, overwhelmed and powerless it's easy to feel that stress, tension and conflict are an inevitable part of family life. It's easy to wonder if things will ever be different.

Things *can* be different—harmony and cooperation *can* prevail in your home—and that's what this book is all about.

Parenting today is difficult and to raise children successfully requires skills and techniques that aren't automatically acquired but can be learned. Other parents have done it, and you can too—no matter how hopeless you may feel the situation is at the moment.

In this book you will learn the skills and words that will enable you to respond to your child's misbehavior in a firm, consistent and loving manner. You will help your child make better behavior choices—and you'll feel better for doing so.

A Practical Guide for Responsible, Caring Discipline

Being a parent is the single most important responsibility you will have in your lifetime. As a parent you are responsible for ensuring your child's health and safety, imparting moral values, teaching appropriate behavior and creating an atmosphere in which your child can flourish physically, emotionally and creatively. Through your constant and loving guidance, your child will learn right from wrong. Through your encouragement, your child will develop confidence and self-esteem. Through your teaching and the examples you set, your child will learn the self-discipline necessary to lead a happy, productive life.

Effective Parenting and Discipline

Although many people equate discipline with punishment—even with spanking or hitting a child—that isn't what discipline means at all. Discipline is not punishment. Discipline is not coming down hard on your child. Rather, discipline is the process of lovingly and with great care teaching your child how to make good behavior choices and how to exercise self-control.

Teaching your child to make better behavior choices is a big responsibility and it may be your greatest challenge. But it can also be your greatest success as you see your child develop sound judgment, responsibility and self-esteem.

Discipline is the art of helping your child develop and mature.

On the pages that follow you will find a four-step plan for guiding your child toward better behavior. The more clearly you understand these steps, the more prepared you'll be to handle the inevitable problems that arise. You'll know what to do when your child refuses to do as he is asked. You'll know how to respond to your child's arguments. You'll know what to say when your child challenges you.

When you can handle these daily crises with confidence, your feelings of powerlessness and frustration will decrease. And most important, your child will learn to make the right behavior choices.

Here are the four steps we will cover:

Communicate assertively.

Perhaps nowhere in life is communication more important than in the relationship between parent and child. To guide your child successfully through the untraveled territory of early life, first you must be able to speak so he will listen. In this step you will learn to recognize the ineffective ways you may be responding to your child now, and how to replace them with more effective responses. By speaking assertively and with confidence you will help to prevent problem behaviors from occuring—no more no-win arguments, non-stop shouting matches or words that are ignored. Once you know how to speak so your child will listen, you'll find that your child will indeed listen to you. And that's the first step toward teaching and encouraging better behavior.

Decide on the behaviors you want from your child.

In this step you will be given guidelines for focusing your attention on the problem behaviors that are most important to you and your child. You will learn how to "pick your battles"—to decide which behaviors are truly the most important to your child's well-being and development and focus on them. You will then be given guidelines for successfully teaching your child to replace inappropriate behaviors with appropriate ones.

Be ready to back up your words with actions.

The key to helping your child understand that what you say is important and meaningful is to be ready with a plan of action. In this step you will be given guidelines for how to respond when your child won't listen to you, or refuses to do as he is asked. You won't have to fall back on angry responses that come from frustration: inappropriate comments, unfair or illogical punishments, meaningless threats or simply backing off. You will be able to give your child an important choice: Choose better behavior or choose to accept the consequences of misbehavior. This is a powerful technique because it places responsibility for what happens right where it belongs—on your child's shoulders.

Take time to make your child feel special—and successful.

There are many opportunities throughout the day to tell your child that what she is doing is terrific and that you are proud of her. This step will show you how to give your child that special positive support that will make her feel good about behaving responsibly and encourage her to choose to repeat these behaviors. Keep in mind as you help your child grow that the goal of discipline is not punishment, but guiding her to make sound, sensible decisions that will ultimately help her be successful.

Communicate assertively.

How many times have you felt that talking to your child was an exercise in futility? If you've ever been criticized, ignored, talked back to, dismissed or yelled at by your child when you asked him to cooperate, do chores, get ready for bed, share, or stop bickering and fighting with siblings, you know the tension it causes.

Words said in anger, frustration or haste are not always what parents intend—the child gets upset and the parent feels guilty and responsible for contributing to an unhappy situation. When parents don't know what else to do or say to get their child to behave, unwanted, unproductive words and feelings are expressed. The way in which you talk to your child when he misbehaves greatly influences how your child will respond to you. Learning how to deliver your message clearly and calmly will give your children an opportunity to learn from a consistent, caring role model, and eventually will influence them to behave in a similar way.

The first thing to understand is how you *really* react when your child misbehaves. There is communication from parents that is effective and gets results, and communication that is ineffective and that may actually encourage your child to continue to misbehave. We have divided the most common ineffective responses into two categories: **nonassertive** and **hostile**. As you read the examples that follow, ask yourself, "Do I ever say anything like this?"

The goal here is to help you recognize if your responses have been ineffective so that in the future you can communicate your concerns to your child in a gentle but firm manner—one that shows your child that you care too much to allow him (or her) to misbehave.

Avoid *nonassertive* responses to your child's misbehavior.

When your child misbehaves, do you tell him clearly and firmly the way you would like him to behave? Or do you respond in a wishy-washy, uncaring or negative manner? Take a look at the nonassertive responses that follow. They are ineffective because the parent is not telling the child exactly how to behave.

**AVOID:
Making
Vague Threats**

Many parents feel that just the threat of being removed from the situation should get results.

Problem: Child is acting silly at the dinner table.

Parent: If you do that one more time, I'll send you to your room.

(*After a few minutes, child begins acting up again*)

Parent: I'm not kidding around. If you can't control yourself, this time you're going to your room.

A child usually knows a bluff when she hears one. After all, she's probably heard the threat so many times before that she's fairly secure that the threat will never be carried out.

**AVOID:
Demanding
Without Following Through**

**AVOID:
Asking
Pointless Questions**

Not following through is a common nonassertive response to misbehavior. In these situations, the parent responds with a firm demand, yet does nothing to make the child comply.

Parent: Billy, stop playing that video game and get your chores done right now! I'm tired of having to talk to you about this.

Child: Okay, Dad. I'll do them.

    (A few minutes later the parent returns and the child is still playing the video game)

Parent: Billy, I told you to do your chores. Now put down that game and do them.

Child: Sorry, Dad. I'll do them right now.

    (Parent again returns in a few minutes and child is still playing with the video game)

Parent: Doggone it, Billy. I told you to stop playing that video game fifteen minutes ago and do your chores! You never listen to me. I've had it with you.

Some parents feel that if they can determine the cause of their children's misbehavior, they can stop it. In theory this principle is sound; in practice it rarely works. Most young children don't know why they are misbehaving and most older children give reasons parents probably won't like.

Many parents ask pointless questions just out of habit. If your child can't supply an answer that will help solve the problem, don't ask it.

For example:

    "Why are you being so mean to your sister?"

    "What have I done to deserve this back talk from you?"

    "Why can't you children sit in the car nicely instead of poking each other?"

    "How many times do I have to tell you to take out the trash before you leave for school?"

What does the parent want the child to say? Five times? Ten times?

Why don't you please try to get along?

AVOID: Begging and Pleading

There's nothing else I can do, so why try?

AVOID: Ignoring the Problem

Many parents feel so overwhelmed that they end up pleading with their children to behave. Negotiating from a position of weakness rarely ensures success.

Child: I don't want to go to bed.

Parent: It's ten o'clock and I'm very tired. Won't you please just go to bed? It's way past your bedtime.

Child: But I'm not tired.

Parent: (*exasperated*) But I am. Please, just go to sleep so I can get some rest.

When parents plead, they are asking their child to feel sorry for them. That is usually not reason enough for a disruptive child to behave.

Some parents feel so inadequate dealing with their children's misbehavior that they ignore it as though it had never occurred.

Problem: A mother and a friend are visiting. The four-year-old daughter continually interrupts, demands her mother's attention and then throws a tantrum and uses inappropriate language until the mother gives the child her undivided attention.

Friend: Doesn't it bother you when your daughter behaves like that and uses four-letter words?

Parent: What can I do? She's just high-strung and if I try to get her to behave, she acts even worse. She won't listen to me. I've given up!

This kind of parent helplessness teaches a child that being a tiny tyrant pays off. She'll always get her way if she's persistent enough with her misbehavior. "Mom can't handle me, so she'll finally give in and I'll get what I want."

AVOID: Yelling from Another Room

Some parents try to discipline from a distance—and it just doesn't work. This is how your child interprets your long-distance demands for behavior: "If my parent was that serious, he'd come in here and tell me to my face. I won't listen until he really means business."

Nonassertive responses can range from indirect statements and firm demands that are not followed through to just ignoring the behavior. What all of these responses have in common is that they don't make the kind of powerful impression that lets your child know that you mean business. Children need parents to assert their authority. To feel secure and loved, they need to know that parents are in charge.

Avoid *hostile* responses to your child's misbehavior.

The second type of ineffective response is hostility. Put-downs, meaningless threats and off-the-wall punishments, because they are emotional and often inappropriate, are an invitation to challenge and anger. Because they disregard a child's feelings, they send a message to the child that says, "I don't like you." The words your child hears from you will become the way he feels about himself. Hostile responses tear down a child's self-esteem and are ultimately damaging.

Most parents don't mean to be hostile. When they don't know how to handle the situation, they become frustrated and lose control, and ugly words and actions follow. Instead, what children need from parents is a consistent, firm and loving attitude if they are to attain the self-esteem and confidence that is crucial to their success in life.

The hostile responses that follow range from inconsiderate comments to cruel, verbal attacks. The degree of severity may differ, but all have two things in common: They will not encourage your child to behave and they must be avoided. As you read, try to be honest with yourself; if you are hostile, recognize it. Only then can you begin to repair the damage with the positive actions we will be addressing later.

AVOID:
Verbal
Put-Downs

AVOID:
Unrealisitic
Threats

Sometimes parents respond to their children's misbehavior with a barrage of angry verbal assaults.

Parent: (*angrily*) I got another note from your teacher today about your school work. You're impossible. Aren't you capable of listening in class? Can't you do anything right? You act as if you belong in kindergarten!

Children often respond to sarcastic remarks with anger and defiance. This is a no-win situation for both parent and child. Sarcasm is insincere and unkind. It has no place in a caring parent's repertoire.

Many parents threaten their children with vague, unrealistic punishments if misbehavior continues. These parents have no intention of following through with these threats. This tactic is an attempt to scare children into submission.

Parent: If you ever talk to me like that again, I'll make you sorry you ever opened your mouth.

Again, these threats sound strong—even frightening—but we have found that most children learn at any early age that phrases such as "If you ever do that again, I'm going to. . . " are usually not enforced by the parents. The children learn to disregard such messages and continue their misbehavior.

AVOID: Out-of-Control Behavior

You're driving me crazy!

Screaming and yelling, turning red in the face, clenching your teeth (or your fists)—all of these hostile responses communicate to your child that you are out of control. These responses may scare your child, but they aren't effective at changing behavior. Why should a child try to control his behavior when a parent is unable to control his own?

AVOID: Severe Punishment

You're grounded for the entire summer.

Severe punishment for misbehavior is usually given when parents are frustrated and haven't given enough thought to the situation. This kind of punishment is a knee-jerk reaction that does nothing to teach the child to make responsible choices.

Parent: Why didn't you call to let us know where you were? We've been worried sick. You are totally irresponsible. You're grounded for the next month.

Child: But that's not fair!

Parent: Life isn't fair, but maybe you'll think twice next time. Just go to your room.

> *I'm going to give you what you deserve.*

AVOID: Physical Response

Parents who resort to physical abuse (pulling hair, squeezing an arm, pinching, slapping or hitting) are not setting limits for their child. These parents are teaching their child that it's all right to hit those you love. They are also teaching their child that resorting to physical abuse is an appropriate way to handle problems.

For example:

Action	Reaction
Mom doesn't like the way I clean my room.	**She slaps me.**
I don't like my brother making fun of me.	**I slap him.**
Dad doesn't like me talking back to him.	**He hits me.**
I don't like my sister grabbing my toys.	**I hit her.**

Other physical responses such as pounding a fist on a table, throwing an object or kicking furniture can be as frightening and destructive to a child as a slap across the face.

Many of the behaviors parents find most annoying in their children are the behaviors children have learned by watching the adults in their lives. Not only does hitting generate more hitting, it also breaks down the all-important lines of communication between parent and child.

Why don't these **hostile, severe responses** work? Children learn that your loud threats and inappropriate punishments indicate that you probably don't have either the will or the way to make them toe the line. Once a child knows this, she will either tune you out, distrust you, challenge you or defy you.

Listen to yourself.

We all use ineffective responses from time to time. Your job now is to learn to listen to yourself when you are speaking to your child and eliminate the nonassertive and hostile responses that are a barrier to growth and understanding. Only then can you develop the new habits that will help you communicate effectively as you guide your child through life.

In the next section you'll learn how to replace your ineffective responses with more effective ones.

Communicate to your child in a caring, assertive manner.

Now that you are aware of the ineffective ways you may be responding to your child's misbehavior, you are ready to learn a more effective approach—one that will improve communication and encourage your child to make better choices about how he will behave. We call this effective approach an **assertive** response.

Learn how to speak so that your child will listen.

Have the lines of communication broken down between you and your child? When you say "no," do you really mean it or can your child coax, coerce or negotiate with you until the "no" becomes a "maybe" and the "maybe" becomes an "okay"? If past experience has taught your child that you don't mean what you say, then all of your efforts to get your child to behave responsibly are doomed to failure.

It's time to adopt a new philosophy: I say what I mean and I mean what I say.

Choose your words carefully—and then stick by them. Your child will quickly learn that you truly care how he behaves if you follow these simple guidelines:

- **Stay calm.** If necessary, count to 10 or begin reciting the alphabet backwards. When you "lose your cool," you lose control and an effective parent must stay in control of the situation.

- **Don't argue or lose your temper.** Don't scream or yell your requests. And never match your child's anger with your own. It's a no-win situation.

- **State what you expect of your child in a firm, direct, nonargumentative manner.** Let your child know that you disapprove of her behavior and then explain exactly what you want her to do:

  For example:

  "It's time for you to go to bed right now."

  "Turn off the television and begin your homework immediately."

  "You need to stay out of your brother's room. It's off limits to you."

These messages leave no doubt in your child's mind what you want her to do. A calm, firm, nonargumentative way of speaking is critical if you want your child to listen to you.

*Guiding your child
with love requires a firm position
and a kind heart.*

Be specific.

When speaking assertively, be specific:
Avoid vague statements such as "act nice,"
"be good" or "act your age." Confident,
clear and direct statements get the best
results.

Avoid asking questions when you really want to make a clear, firm statement.

Don't say, "How about feeding the dog
now?" Your child might respond with an
all-too-familiar delaying tactic such as: "I
will after I watch my program." If you
want your child to feed the dog now, make
your request in a calm, assertive voice:
"You need to feed the dog now."

Get close.

When you need to speak to your child, get
close and speak calmly. Don't yell from
across the room or from another part of
the house. When your child misbehaves,
walk over to her, make eye contact and
state calmly exactly what you want.

Here are examples of two types of
responses: ineffective and assertive.
Notice the difference in not only the words
chosen, but in the approach as well.

Ineffective Response

Child: (*throwing toys at her sister*)

Parent: (*yelling from another room*)
          Please leave your sister alone.
          You're driving me crazy. Don't
          make me come in there because
          you'll get it if I hear one more
          peep from either of you.

Assertive Response

Child: (*throwing toys at her sister*)

          (*Parent comes into room, walks
          up to the child and speaks
          calmly*)

Parent: Throwing toys is not allowed.
          Do not throw toys at your
          sister or at anyone else.

Don't beg. Don't get angry.

Don't become exasperated. Instead, when
making a request of your child, be calm
and use direct statements that send this
message:

"This is what I expect you to do."

Here are some more examples of how to speak so your child will listen:

Problem: It's almost dinner time and your child has his toys scattered all over the floor.

Parent: Start cleaning up your toys, son. Dinner is almost ready.

Child: (*continuing to play*) I'll pick them up after dinner.

(*Walk over to your child, look him straight in the eyes and speak calmly*)

Parent: I understand you want to continue playing, but it's dinner time, so you need to put these toys away.

Problem: It's 8:00 p.m. and you're sitting in the living room reading the newspaper. Your daughter is in her bedroom, talking on the phone.

Parent: (*calling to daughter*) It's getting late. Have you finished your homework yet?

Child: (*yelling back*) No. I'm on the phone.

(*Walk calmly into your daughter's room, sit down on the bed next to her, look her straight in the eye and speak quietly*)

Parent: Your homework must be finished before you go to bed. You need to hang up the phone now and finish your homework.

It's not only what you say, it's how you say it.

Here are some guidelines for body language that gets your message across loud and clear.

Look your child in the eye when you speak.

You can say as much with your eyes as with your words, so establish eye contact when speaking with your child. This technique will be especially helpful if your child is easily distracted. If your child won't look at you, gently turn her head until your eyes meet. Then praise her for looking at you.

Use hand gestures to add emphasis to your words.

Hand gestures can be used to emphasize what you are saying. Make sure your hand gestures don't intimidate your child. Pointing a finger in your child's face will do nothing more than frighten him or make him angry.

Touch your child.

Placing your hand gently on your child's shoulder as you speak is a clear indicator of the sincerity and forcefulness of your message. This gesture should be a gentle way to focus your child's attention on you. Don't squeeze, pinch or hurt your child.

What to Do When Your Child Argues with You

Why does a child argue? As children grow, they make continual attempts to be independent from their parents. At all stages of development, in different ways on different days, they try to make their own decisions. They are trying to see how far they can go with their own wants and needs, and if they go too far they need to be guided gently back on track. Some children learn that if they are persistent enough with resisting your requests—if they argue—you will finally back down and give in, or be sidetracked and forget the problem at hand. Here's what we mean:

Problem: It's 8:30 p.m.—Kathy's bedtime. She is playing a video game.

Parent: Kathy, don't you think it's time to get ready for bed?

Child: No, I'm not tired yet. Just let me pass this level. I'm almost there.

Parent: (*pleading*) But you've been playing with that game all night. Now please get ready for bed.

Child: Why do you always do this to me? Just when I'm ready to win, you make me go to bed. Kara's mother lets her stay up until nine o'clock.

Parent: (*exasperated*) Maybe Kara doesn't need as much sleep as you do. I never can get you up on time in the morning if you don't get enough sleep. Can't you please just do as I ask and turn off that video game?

Child: It really doesn't matter if I go to bed now or in five minutes and in five minutes I can finish my game. Give me a break, okay?

Parent: (*angrily*) Kathy, you know that it's never only five minutes with you and if you keep arguing with me I'll get rid of that game. I've told you that before and this time I really mean it!

What happened here? By arguing—by getting into a pointless discussion—the parent has lost control of the situation. Kathy is still playing the game. She has not started getting ready for bed. And the frustrated parent has resorted to meaningless threats that the child has heard many times before—threats that have never been carried out.

What should you do in a situation like this? Don't argue. Use the "broken record" technique! Let's turn the page and see how this technique can really help you take control and avoid arguments.

The "Broken Record" Technique

When your child refuses to comply with your request ("Go to bed," "Pick up your toys," "Start your homework") or will not accept no for an answer ("No, you may not have a candy bar," "No, you can't watch TV while you're doing your homework"), don't argue or get angry or give in.

Instead, very clearly tell your child what you want her to do. If she argues, simply repeat the statement—like a broken record that keeps repeating the same phrase. No matter how much your child argues, complains or contests, respond calmly and repeat your expectation. Depending on how successful your child has been in the past at resisting your requests, it may take several repetitions before she complies. Eventually, though, she will see that you're not changing your statement—or your mind.

Here's how the broken-record technique works:

Parent: Kathy, it's time to get ready for bed. Turn the game off. [**Statement of want**]

Child: (*playing her video game*) I'm not tired yet. Just let me pass this level. I'm almost there.

Parent: (*in a calm but firm voice*) It's time for you to get ready for bed. Turn the game off now. [**Broken record**]

Child: Why *do* you always *do* this to me? Just when I'm about ready to win, you make me go to bed. Kara's mother lets her stay up until nine o'clock.

Parent: (*remaining calm*) I understand that you want to continue playing, but you've been having trouble getting up in the morning so you need to turn off the game and get ready for bed now. [**Broken record**]

Child: If you let me stay up just five more minutes, I'll go to bed fifteen minutes earlier tomorrow night. Please?

Parent: I hear what you are saying, Kathy, but you need to turn off the game and get ready for bed now. [**Broken record**]

Child: Oh, all right. I hear you.

By staying firm—not arguing and not getting sidetracked—chances are good that your child will do what you have asked. She may grumble and complain, but she now knows that you really mean what you are saying.

Guidelines for using the broken record:

1. **Determine what you want** your child to do. "I want you to pick up your toys."

2. **Keep repeating what you want** when your child argues with you. Do not respond to any statement from your child.

3. Use the broken record three times.

If your child still does not do what you want, be prepared to back up your words with actions (as we will discuss in Step 3). For example:

Parent: Ken, stop hitting your brother. [**Statement of want**]

Child: It's not my fault. He was making weird faces at me.

Parent: (*firmly*) I'll talk to him about it. But you listen to what I'm saying to you: Stop hitting your brother. [**Broken record**]

Child: You always take his side. If he does it again, I'm going to punch him.

Parent: I understand you're upset, but you may not hit your brother. [**Broken record**]

Child: You can't make me. I'll do what I want!

Parent: (*calmly*) Ken, you must stop hitting your brother. [**Broken record**] You have a choice: Leave your brother alone or you will be grounded until bedtime. [*Being prepared to back up your words with actions*]

Child: That's not fair. I hate living here.

A Final Thought

Once you master the caring, assertive communication skills presented in Step 1, you will be able to resolve many of the problems causing stress and friction between you and your child.

Just remember, **learning to speak assertively won't happen overnight**. It may take a while, but success is attainable if you make a conscious effort to practice these new skills every day. **Listen to yourself** when you speak to your child or ask a spouse or other adult to listen and evaluate the way you speak.

- Are you speaking assertively, but with a kind, caring tone?

- Have you stopped asking pointless questions or making hostile, sarcastic remarks that have no positive impact on changing your child's behavior?

- Are you learning to ignore your child's manipulations (whining, crying, making unpleasant comments such as "I hate you")?

Communicate with caring and authority. If you do this consistently, your child will become more focused on behaving appropriately and less focused on what he is doing wrong.

Decide on the behaviors you want from your child.

It's inevitable! Parents and children are going to disagree—sooner or later. From the time your child first learns how to exert his will and express his desires and opinions, some degree of conflict is unavoidable and normal. If these conflicts are left unresolved or are resolved with anger and hostility, they can be destructive and harmful to your child's self-esteem. On the other hand, if your child's behavior is guided with the care and consistency that comes from knowing what to do and what to say, you will be constructive and helpful in teaching your child responsibility and self-control.

If your child is to grow successfully into adulthood, he must make some of his own decisions about how he behaves. So then how do you decide which behaviors you as a responsible parent are supposed to shape, and which to overlook? The best way is to start with a few fundamental rules for the family, rules that all family members are expected to observe. After that, you must decide for yourself what kind of misbehavior violates your values, your sense of fairness, or the growth or health of your children.

Determine your basic family rules.

Some problems can be prevented by creating a set of family rules—a basic framework from which your family can operate. These are spoken (or unspoken) rules in your family concerning how family members should treat one another. Even though your family may have a general understanding of what the rules are, it is important to take a closer look at these indispensable guidelines for behavior.

Everyone in a family has the right to live without the threat of physical harm or verbal abuse. Everyone deserves to be treated with respect. You may believe that your children know these basic rules without your having to state them, but that may not be the case. So that everybody in the family has the greatest opportunity to observe what you believe are the most necessary requirements for living harmoniously, write the rules down and make them nonnegotiable and ongoing.

Choose rules that will help minimize normal, everyday problems.

If physical fighting is a continuing problem in your home, make a rule about fighting. If name-calling is a constant source of irritation, outlaw it. If your child speaks disrespectfully to others or gives little consideration to the property or privacy of other family members, then create rules for these ongoing misbehaviors.

Make rules specific.

Your rules will be easier to comply with and enforce if they are specific. Vague rules such as "Don't treat your sister unkindly" or "Always be nice" can lead to confusion. What a parent considers as unkind or nice behavior may be defined quite differently by a seven-year-old child.

Here is an example of a family's list of rules:

Family Rules

1. Don't hit, bite, pinch or kick others.

2. Speak respectfully to others (no name-calling).

3. Ask permission before using someone else's possessions.

Family rules apply to everyone in the family.

Don't expect your child to abide by family rules that you do not plan to follow too. The behavior you model is the behavior your child will ultimately emulate. If the rule is no hitting, then no one should be physically abusive to anyone else. No spousal shoving matches. No spankings for unruly children. If the rule is no name-calling, then parents must follow suit— with children and spouses alike.

Decide on the consequences for breaking the rules.

Consequences for breaking rules might include "time out" (separation from others into a nonstimulating situation), losing privileges, or grounding. (See Step 3 for specific information about choosing and providing consequences.)

Explain the rules at a family meeting.

Once the rules are chosen, write them on a sheet of paper. Then gather the family together for a special meeting. Discuss each rule, talk about why it's important and what will happen if a rule is broken.

Focus on changing those behaviors that cause conflict in your home.

To start your child off in a positive direction, you have determined and listed your family rules—the three or four most important rules that everyone in the family is expected to observe. But obviously these rules don't cover all the situations that present themselves daily in family life. Other issues that are certainly worth your attention and guidance are:

- coming home on time,
- doing assigned chores,
- respecting the property of others,
- speaking with consideration, and
- kindness.

However, matters such as hanging up the bathroom towel or eating everything on the plate may not be the places to draw the line.

Pick your battles.

If you fight with your child frequently, you are probably trying to control too many aspects of her life. If your child is to learn to be self-reliant and develop into a responsible young person, she must be able to make some decisions on her own. They may not always be the decisions you would make, and they may not always be in your child's best interest, but in the long run making her own decisions about the smaller issues will help her grow as much as your guidance will through the larger issues.

Therefore, you need to pick your battles and concentrate your efforts on the issues you can't put on the back burner and ignore. What does your child do, or not do, that drives you crazy? What do you fight with your child about on a regular basis?

Use the chart on the following page to help you pinpoint the behaviors that you'd like to focus your attention on.

PICK YOUR BATTLES

Place a check by those behaviors you need your child to change—now.
If you don't find your specific problem on the list, fill it in at the bottom.

❏ **household responsibilities**
(cleaning own room, dirty clothes not put in hamper, chores not completed in a timely manner or to your specification)

❏ **bad attitude**
(toward parents, siblings, others)

❏ **fighting with siblings**
(minor squabbles, constant arguing and bickering, hitting, biting, kicking)

❏ **bedtime battles**
(dawdling, refusing to go to bed)

❏ **morning problems**
(hard to get up, always late)

❏ **homework**
(getting started, giving assignments his/her best effort, doing work independently)

❏ **car trouble**
(squabbling with siblings, refusal to wear seat belt, complaining)

❏ **lying**
(white lies to big whoppers)

❏ **too much TV, video games**

❏ **bad manners**
(at the table, when playmates or family friends are visiting, at holiday gatherings and annual family events)

❏ **poor eating habits**
(junk-food junkie, refuses to eat what you serve)

❏ **not following directions**
(curfew, phone privileges)

❏ **talking back**

❏ **bad language**

❏ **tantrums**
(at home, away from home)

❏ **whining**

❏ **name-calling**

❏ **teasing**

❏ **tattling**

❏ **interrupting**

❏ _____

Once you have "picked your battles," focus on the behavior you want to work on first. By choosing one, you're not dismissing the others. You can deal with all of the problems in time, but for now you need to concentrate your efforts on changing only one behavior. Once you and your child have successfully worked out this problem, the others will be easier to handle. Both of you will have put into action some of the new habits it takes to change behavior.

Your child will know, perhaps for the first time, that you care too much to let her misbehave, that you will consistently follow through, and that there will be consequences if the behavior doesn't change. And she'll know that when she does behave, you will recognize it with praise and other positive actions. Your mutual success in working through this first problem will mark the beginning of an improved relationship.

Teach your child how to behave appropriately.

Guideline #1

Teach your child exactly how you expect him to behave.

First, think about the problem behavior and the situations during which the misbehavior usually takes place. Then ask yourself, "How do I want my child to act in these situations?" Once you have decided what your child needs to do to change his behavior, show him exactly what you expect. Don't take anything for granted. Be specific.

Here is a typical behavior problem and an example of how parents might teach their child how to behave appropriately when riding in the car:

Every time you get into the car your children start bickering and fighting with each other. In the past you've yelled at the kids to calm down and threatened to turn the car around and go home if they didn't behave, but usually your requests fell on deaf ears and the sibling squabbles continued until one or both of them grew bored with their antics. First of all, this kind of behavior is not in your children's best interests. Accidents happen when the driver's attention is not completely focused on the road. It's your responsibility to show your children how you expect them to behave in the car—every time you go for a drive.

A. Take your children aside and explain what you want.

Parent: Whenever we are driving in the car, I need to be able to concentrate on driving safely. It is important to all of us that you both behave. No bickering. No fighting. No yelling. This will be the rule whenever you are in a car—our car, the carpool, or when driving with your friend's parents.

B. Describe specifically what your children need to do.

When you state your expectations, keep them simple and easy to understand.

Parent: Whenever we go in the car, first you will buckle your seat belt. You must sit there calmly and keep your hands and feet to yourself. Don't yell or scream. If you like, you may read a book or a magazine or play a game from the activity box.

TIP Some problems can be solved by planning ahead. If your children fight when they are bored, keep a book bag or activity box (filled with books, games, paper, pencils, story cassettes) in the car. When your children start getting restless (in the car, at the doctor's office, at a friend's house), break open the book bag.

C. Be sure your children understand what is expected of them.

Ask your children to review how you expect them to behave whenever they go in the car. It may help to ask them to pretend they are in the car and to show you how they would buckle their seat belt, keep their hands and feet to themselves and play quietly with items from the activity box. Emphasize that these rules must be followed all the time. Show your confidence that your children can do what you expect. Be positive.

D. Explain what will happen if they don't change their behavior.

You must be ready with a plan of action if your children don't follow these rules. The consequences may seem time-consuming and more bothersome to you than to your children, but if you follow through consistently each time they misbehave, it will be time well spent.

Parent: If you begin fighting while I'm driving, I'll pull over to the side of the road until you stop. At the end of the trip you will have a time-out in the car.

Guideline #2
Give gentle reminders about what you expect.

One way to help your child succeed is to remind him of proper behavior—before encountering situations that could cause problems. Here's what we mean:

- If your child usually misbehaves at the market, remind him of how you expect him to behave *before* you go to the market.

  "When we go to the market today, I want you to sit in the grocery cart quietly. Don't take things from the shelves unless I ask you to. When we are in the checkout line, do not ask for candy or gum. If you behave as I expect you to at the market, we will play a game at home after I put the groceries away."

- If your daughter procrastinates about doing her homework, remind her to do her homework early *before* it becomes an issue.

  "I know your favorite television program is on tonight, so please have your homework completed before eight o'clock."

- If your son has a problem making his curfew, remind him of his curfew *before* he leaves the house.

  "I don't want you to have to be grounded again so make sure you're home no later than ten o'clock tonight."

Guideline #3
Plan ahead to avoid problems.

Some problems can be eliminated with a little pre-planning. If your child misbehaves because she is bored or wants your attention, give her something to focus her attention away from misbehavior. Here's what we mean:

- If your daughter acts up in restaurants, be prepared before you go out to eat. Place toys, puzzles, coloring books and crayons in a small box or bag. Before entering the restaurant, explain exactly how you expect her to behave.

  "While we are in the restaurant, I want you to stay in your chair. At the table you may use anything from the toy bag, as long as you do it quietly. Keep your hands and feet to yourself, and use your best manners when you are eating."

- If you receive an important phone call and don't want to be interrupted, excuse yourself from the caller for half a minute while you explain your expectations to your child.

  "I need to speak on the phone for ten minutes. Remember not to interrupt me while I'm talking. Why don't you play with your game or read a book while I'm on the phone."

Guideline #4
Be realistic about your expectations.

A three-year-old child shouldn't be expected to sit quietly through a seven-course, two-hour meal. Young children will probably become anxious and irritable when traveling long distances. Gauge your child's limits and make changes as necessary. Get a babysitter if your child can't sit through a long restaurant meal. Make frequent stops on long car trips.

Guideline #5
Use positive reinforcement to encourage continued good behavior.

Praise your child for getting through the experience without misbehaving.

"You were so well-behaved at Aunt Carol's today. I knew you could do it. We'll go for another visit soon."

"Our family really enjoyed dinner tonight. Because you and your brother got along so nicely, we all had fun."

STEP 3

Be ready to back up your words with actions.

When your child behaves according to your requests, he has made a growth step in the right direction, and you will give him plenty of loving praise to keep him on track. However, situations in which your child does not do what you have asked could also prove to be fertile ground for growth if you follow through and handle the misbehavior immediately.

In any situation, be prepared for your child to test you to see if you really mean what you say. Don't fail this test by ignoring the misbehavior. To show your child how much it means to you that he behave, you must take action as soon as possible.

Choose appropriate disciplinary consequences.

Your action will take the form of providing your child with an appropriate consequence for choosing *not* to follow the rule.

For example:

Your son fights with his younger sibling on the way to soccer practice.

Consequence: You pull the car to the side of the road and wait until he stops fighting. Once you reach soccer practice, he must remain in the car for a five-minute time out before going to practice.

Your daughter comes home fifteen minutes after her curfew.

Consequence: Her curfew is rolled back an hour earlier for the next week.

Caring parents know that it is necessary to teach a growing child what the outcome of his behavior will be. This is best learned by allowing the child to choose the result of his actions: He can behave well, knowing he will benefit; or he can misbehave, knowing that the results will be something he will not like.

Be prepared for your child's inevitable testing by choosing appropriate consequences *ahead of time.* As soon as you have assertively told your child what you want her to do and you anticipate that she may not comply, ask yourself this question: "What will I do if my child doesn't listen to me?" In other words, there and then you need to know exactly how you are going to back up your words with actions to ensure that your child behaves.

You may want to discuss these consequences with your spouse. You should both be in total agreement about what will happen if your child chooses to misbehave—no matter which parent is present. If time out is the consequence for hitting a sibling, both parents should be ready and willing to provide the consequence when the misbehavior occurs.

Providing consequences is a reasonable and effective way to motivate your child to behave. Follow these guidelines for choosing appropriate consequences:

Guideline #1
Consequences should be logically related to the problem behavior.

A consequence that, whenever possible, is logically related to the misbehavior is useful because it teaches your child to take responsibility for his own actions. Our daily lives (and our children's lives) are sometimes filled with unpleasant consequences because of the actions we have chosen to take. For example, if we bake in the hot sun without sunscreen, we receive an uncomfortable sunburn; if we return library books late, we pay a fine. Sometimes it takes more than one sunburn or more than one late fee to make us change our behavior. But eventually the lesson does sink in.

The same is true for children. If your child learns that the consequence for throwing toys is losing the privilege of using those toys, she will eventually stop throwing the toys if she really wants to play with them. These consequences, however, are successful at changing behavior only if you use them *every time your child misbehaves*.

Here are some common problems and the logical consequences which, when given consistently, can help change problem behavior:

Your ten-year-old fights with neighborhood friends.
Logical Consequence: Child is grounded inside the house for a day.

Your sixteen-year-old uses the car without your permission.
Logical Consequence: Revoke car privileges for a week.

Your fourteen-year-old daughter continually plays the stereo too loudly in her room.
Logical Consequence: Give your daughter a choice: Turn down the stereo or have it removed from her room for one week.

Your four-year-old son hits his sister for touching his toy.
Logical Consequence: Give your son a four-minute time out (one minute for each year of age) and make that toy off limits to him for a day.

Your seven-year-old leaves the house without telling you.
Logical Consequence: You ground the child at home for the following two days.

Guideline #2
Choose consequences that your child won't like, but that are not harmful.

Any disciplinary consequence, to be effective, must be something your child does not particularly enjoy. A preschooler probably will not enjoy being sent to his room for five or ten minutes, but a typical teen may like being sent to her room where she can entertain herself with TV, music or video games. A seven-year-old might not mind losing the privilege of talking on the phone with friends, but your teenager might be horrified at the prospect of having you cut off that link to her friends.

No one knows your child better than you do, so choose consequences that will be meaningful enough to encourage your child to do as you ask rather than choose the consequence. Keep in mind that while these disciplinary consequences should not be enjoyable to your child, neither should they be physically or emotionally harmful to your child.

Here are some common problems and consequences that most children would find unpleasant.

Child hates to get up in the morning; whines and complains.

Consequence: Child goes to bed fifteen minutes earlier each evening until he is able to get up on time without whining and complaining.

Children fight over video games.

Consequence: Remove video game from house for several days.

Child teases sibling, calling her names.

Consequence: Time-out away from family for ten minutes.

These disciplinary consequences may not seem that unpleasant to you, but to a child or teen, they could be just the right motivation to stop misbehaving.

We have divided the most common and effective disciplinary consequences into three categories: separation (or time out), loss of privileges and grounding.

Separation

This type of consequence is often referred to as "time out." During time out your child is separated from you and others into a nonstimulating, "boring" situation. The child's bedroom, a guest room or the patio are all options. Your child should not be allowed to watch TV, listen to music or play games while separated from the rest of the family.

> **TIP** Set a kitchen timer and place it in the room so your child will know when her time out is finished.

Don't choose a frightening or scary time-out place. Never put your child in a closet, a garage or in any place where he feels unsafe or can get into trouble. Time out isn't meant to punish or frighten your child. It's meant to give him time to think.

Loss of Privileges

Suspend those privileges your child really enjoys such as watching TV, playing outside, talking on the phone, listening to music or playing with special toys. This consequence is especially effective when used consistently. If your child truly believes that every time she misbehaves a privilege will be taken away, she will be more likely to behave appropriately.

Grounding

"You're grounded!" This phrase is universally disliked by most children—and therefore, it can be very effective. When you ground your child for misbehavior, you are restricting him to the yard, house or room for a specific amount of time. This is a logical consequence if your child doesn't follow your rules about curfew, doesn't let you know where he is (when playing away from home or after school) or is aggressive or hostile with others.

> **TIP** Don't let the anger of the moment influence the amount of time you ground your child. Breaking curfew once doesn't demand grounding for a month. You can, however, advise your child that if she breaks her curfew a second time, you will add additional time to grounding. This gives your child fair warning and if she chooses to break curfew again, she chooses to be grounded for a longer time.

Guideline #3
Consequences should be provided as a choice.

Giving a child a choice to behave or to receive a consequence can be a significant aspect of his development. A parent interested in his child's success will state what the choice is and allow the child the freedom to make that choice. The child will grow up understanding that all kinds of opportunities and choices await him even outside of family life, and that good choices bring good results.

When you provide your child with the choice as to whether or not a disciplinary consequence will occur, you place the responsibility where it belongs—on your child.

For example:

Parent: Aaron, I cannot allow you to bother your brother at the dinner table. If you poke or hit your brother one more time, you will choose to sit in your room while we eat. It's your choice.

Child: (*grumbling*) Okay.
(*Gradually Aaron begins to poke his brother under the table again*)

Parent: (*calmly but firmly*) Aaron, you poked your brother again so you have chosen to go to your room and sit there for the remainder of dinner.

The child has made the decision: He has chosen to poke his brother; thus, he has chosen to go to his room.

When you give your child choices, you are providing him with the opportunity to learn the natural consequences of his actions and that he is the one responsible for his own behavior.

TIP Don't back down! If the consequence is to go to his room for the remainder of the meal, don't go into the room in a few minutes and say, "Well, I bet you've learned your lesson. You can come back to the table now." Let him stay there the entire time. When the dinner is over, go to his room and bring him back to the table to finish his meal alone. If staying in his room was an unpleasant, boring consequence, he may choose to behave appropriately at dinner tomorrow rather than choose this consequence again.

Giving your child a choice
to behave or to receive a consequence
teaches responsibility.

Put consequences into action.

Because you will be using consequences to help your child make better choices about her misbehavior, you will want them to have a profound effect. Therefore, once you have decided which consequence you will use, you need to know how best to use it. Here are some guidelines:

Guideline #1
Consequences should be provided as soon as possible.

When your child doesn't listen to you and continues to misbehave, immediately notify her of the disciplinary consequences. You may enforce the consequence at that time.

Parent: Janet, this isn't the time to be on the phone. It's time to do your homework.

Child: (*whining*) But I haven't talked to Brian all day long.

Parent: Janet, you know the rule. No phone calls until your homework is finished. Now say good-bye and get to work.

On the other hand, you may inform your child of a consequence that will occur in the future:

Problem: Child arrives home late for the second day in a row after not telling parent where he would be.

Child: Hi, Dad.

Parent: (*sitting down with child*) Danny, I told you that I'm not comfortable with you going out without letting me know where you will be. I told you yesterday that if you did it again, you would choose to be grounded.

Child: But, Dad, I'm really sorry.

Parent: No buts, Danny. I have to know where you are going. Because you didn't listen to me, you have chosen to be grounded tomorrow afternoon.

Guideline #2
Consequences should be provided every time your child chooses to misbehave.

If you want to be successful at changing your child's behavior you must be consistent. Every time your child chooses to misbehave, you must provide a consequence. No disciplinary consequence will work unless your child is completely certain that you will use it as promised.

Problem: Friends are visiting. Seven-year-old Michelle begins jumping on the furniture. Her mother excuses herself from the company and takes Michelle to another room.

Parent: (*in a calm, assertive manner*) Michelle, jumping on the furniture is not permitted. I want you to stop. If you would like to visit, please come in and sit down. If you would rather play, you may. But you may not jump on the furniture. If you jump again, you'll have to go to your room.

Child: (whining) But I don't want to go to my room.

Parent: Then don't jump on the furniture again.

(After behaving herself for fifteen minutes, Michelle runs into the room and leaps onto the sofa. The mother quietly excuses herself again, takes Michelle by the hand and leads her to her bedroom.)

Parent: Because you have chosen to jump on the furniture again, you have also chosen to stay in your room. I'm setting the timer for ten minutes. If you would like to come back after the timer rings, and you think you can be with us without jumping around, you may. But if you start jumping again, you'll have to return to your room for a longer time-out. It's your decision, Michelle.

Child: (angrily) You're so mean. I hate you.

Parent: Well, I really love you too much to allow you to misbehave.

(Michelle comes out after the timer rings, sulks a bit but behaves herself for about half an hour and then begins jumping again. The mother takes Michelle to her room again.)

Parent: Because you have chosen to jump on the furniture again, Michelle, this time you must stay in your room for twenty minutes.

Many children feel that they can get away with misbehavior when friends or relatives are visiting because they think their parents will be too busy or embarrassed to handle the problem in front of guests. Don't fall into this trap. Consistency will lead to success.

The Importance of Being Consistent

We cannot emphasize enough how important it is for you to follow through with consequences whenever your child misbehaves. Some parents ease off when they see some positive changes in their children's behavior for a few days. But if you relax your efforts, old problems will gradually reappear and soon your child will be misbehaving again.

Consistency is the key to effective discipline. Nothing will work unless parents are prepared to back up their words with actions each and every time their children choose to misbehave. The message you send by being consistent is this: "I love you too much to allow you to misbehave without my responding."

Guideline #3
Consequences should be provided in a matter-of-fact, nonhostile manner.

To discipline your child effectively, you must remain calm. Being hostile, angry or sarcastic will only serve to provoke more misbehavior. When the child feels attacked, his urge will be to fight back.

Talking to your child in a calm, matter-of-fact way may seem like an impossible task, especially when your child has done something particularly disturbing (like talking back or using unacceptable language), but you can remain in control if you follow these simple suggestions:

- Stop what you are doing and silently count to five.
- Plan what you will say.
- Take a deep breath and in a calm voice, clearly state your expectations.
- If necessary, lower your voice and speak slowly.

Problem: Thirteen-year-old Jim has just punched his little sister in the arm as he walked past her.

Parent: (*speaking very slowly and calmly*) Jim, hitting is not permitted in this house.

Jim: (*snarling*) Leave me alone. Why is everyone always on my case around here? I hate living here.

Parent: (*feeling his anger rise, takes a deep breath, and calmly, firmly and slowly continues*) I hear that you are upset, Jim, but you cannot hit your sister.

When you speak slowly, your voice naturally goes lower, which helps to defuse the tension between you and your child. When you speak quickly and angrily, your voice often rises to a higher pitch, causing feelings to escalate. Slow down and stay calm.

> **TIP** Use the "higher/lower" technique when your child argues with you. The higher your child raises his voice, the lower and softer you respond. Nothing captures a child's attention more than when he thinks he will upset you by yelling and mouthing off and you respond in a calm, quiet voice.

Guideline #4
If the consequence does not work, change it.

Let's be realistic. Sometimes your child will continue to misbehave despite the consequence. If this happens, consider these two facts: First, the consequence you have chosen apparently isn't effective enough to stop your child's misbehavior and, second, perhaps your child actually enjoys the attention she gets from you more than she dislikes the consequence for misbehaving.

When you come upon this stumbling block, reassess the situation. Select a different consequence and then make sure you give your child attention for what she is doing *right*, not what she is doing wrong.

Problem: Parent is helping older child with homework in the family room. Ten-year-old Ben starts making a racket with his toys.

Parent: Ben, your sister and I are working on her homework. It needs to be quiet so that we can concentrate. You can play in here as long as you do it quietly.

(*Ben plays quietly for only a few minutes, then begins playing loudly again*)

Parent: Ben, I want you to stop making so much noise with your toys. Your sister and I can't concentrate with all that noise. If you continue to make noise, I will have to take those toys away from you. Do you understand?

Child: Yeah, I guess.

(*Within a few minutes, Ben is firing a laser pistol and making explosion noises*)

Parent: Ben, that pistol is too distracting. Please give it to me.

Child: (*mumbling*) Boy, I can't do a thing around here.

(*After ten minutes, Ben begins playing with a motorized truck which again distracts parent and older sibling*)

Parent: Ben, that truck makes entirely too much noise. Now give me the truck and play with something that doesn't make noise.

(*Ben starts playing with building blocks, but within minutes he's smashing them together loudly*)

Parent: Ben, stop making all that noise with those blocks. Please give them to me now.

What happened here? Even though the parent consistently followed through and took the toys away, Ben continued to make noise. It then became necessary for the parent to try a different consequence.

Parent: Ben, you have a choice. You can either play quietly in here with your toys or you will have to go outside to play.

Don't give in when your child tries to test you.

As we have said before, it is natural and normal for your child to try to make his way as independently as he can through his growing-up years. He will be testing you frequently to see how far he can go—to see what his limits are. Once your child is aware that you aren't wavering from the standards you have set for appropriate behavior, he may become resentful or angry. Some children even resort to tantrums, crying, screaming "I don't love you" or refusing to talk at all when they realize Mom and Dad aren't going to back down.

As difficult as it may be, you must ignore the "I hate you's" and other personal attacks. Let your child know, in no uncertain terms, that you don't like the behavior he is exhibiting—but that you do love him.

The testing will work only if you feel guilty about what you are doing. Remind yourself that it is in your child's best interest that you follow through with the consequences you have imposed. Twenty years from now your child will thank you for not crumbling under the pressure.

For single parents

Many single parents find their children trying to test them with statements such as, "I'd rather live with Dad. He's not mean like you," or "Mom doesn't make me go to bed early when I'm at her house. I hate living with you!" Sometimes children of single parents will try to play one parent against the other. Don't give in to these manipulations.

Forgive and forget.

Once your child has received a consequence, let her express her feelings about the problem and discuss how she might better handle it in the future. Let your child know you love her and have confidence in her ability to improve her behavior.

Problem: Child has been sent to her room for a ten-minute time out for teasing her brother and calling him names.

Parent: (*entering child's room*) Your time out is up. I really don't like keeping you in your room, but I care about you so much that I want you to learn to be respectful of others.

Child: But, Mom, he can be such a brat.

Parent: I understand that you don't always get along with your brother, but teasing and name-calling are just not allowed in our home. I'm confident that you can live with your brother without resorting to teasing or name-calling.

It's very important to praise your child as soon as you see her behaving appropriately (for example, getting along with her brother). Don't overdo the praise, but take her aside and say, "I'm pleased to see you getting along with your brother. I knew you could."

Take time to make your child feel special—and successful.

Be a positive role model!

The goal of discipline is to teach, not to punish. And the very best way to teach your child to behave appropriately is to set an example for your child by behaving in the same way you would like her to behave. The values you embrace and the actions you demonstrate in your everyday life will affect the way your child relates to you and to others.

- Your child will learn to be respectful if he is treated respectfully.
- Your child will learn to be fair if she is treated fairly.
- Your child will learn to be confident if he is given encouragement.

Catch your child being good.

Besides being a model for good behavior, the most effective way you can build good behavior is by giving your child the attention he wants—and needs—when he does behave appropriately. It's so easy to focus attention on the things our children do wrong and to ignore their good behavior. You can reverse this habit (just as you can change the ineffective ways you may be responding to your child) by first paying special attention to the way you interact with your child.

Ask yourself:

- You have had to discipline your child for talking back to you. *What do you do when he is cooperative?*

- You've had to deal with your children continually arguing and fighting with each other. *What do you say when they play together quietly and cooperatively?*

- Your child is a constant problem at school. *How do you respond when you get a good report from the teacher?*

Unfortunately, many parents do not seize the moment and respond with a positive word or action when their child behaves. They do not realize that their child's emotional well-being and self-confidence are directly related to the feedback he receives from his parent.

When your child's behavior improves (even slightly), don't take it for granted. Boost your child's self-esteem and reinforce the good behavior with a warm smile and some caring words of encouragement. For example:

- If your son leaves home without telling you, applaud his behavior when he asks permission to leave.

- If your child usually whines and complains at the market, praise her when she is cooperative.

- If your son has tantrums when he doesn't get his way, encourage him with praise when he cooperates and follows your directions.

*Being a positive
role model is the best gift you
can give your child.*

Use praise to acknowledge improvement and encourage good behavior.

The most powerful form of positive encouragement is praise. How do you feel when you receive praise from a boss, friend or spouse? You're probably inspired to "keep up the good work" or "try a little harder." Your child needs this same kind of encouragement and inspiration—and what better way to show your child how much you appreciate his efforts than with some kind, sincere, thoughtful words.

"You did a great job picking up your toys and putting them in the toy chest. Your room looks so neat and tidy."

"You should feel proud of yourself for behaving so well while our guests were here."

"Good job putting your seat belt on when you got in the car. You buckled it so quickly."

"I appreciate you calling me and letting me know where you were going."

"Thanks for taking out the trash."

Some Pointers about Praise

Here are some suggestions to keep in mind when praising your child.

Praise the behavior.
Tell your child specifically what he is doing, or has done, that you like. Praise your child's accomplishment, not his personality. Avoid vague comments such as "nice going" or "good boy."

Vague: You're a good girl, Jennifer.

Specific: I like the way you asked permission to go to Michelle's house.

Get close when you praise.
Don't yell your approval from across the room. Walk up to your child, look her in the eye and deliver your praise in a friendly, sincere voice.

Praise is no place for sarcasm.
When you praise your child, watch out that you don't pair your praise with a hostile, sarcastic remark. The quickest way to turn your child off is to couple your positive comments with negative "hooks."

Wrong: I like the way you cleaned up today. It's about time.

Wrong: Thanks for helping your sister. I didn't think you had it in you.

Wrong: You were so good today. I can't believe you acted so nice.

These digs are poorly veiled hostilities on the part of frustrated parents.

Super Praise

Super praise is one of the most powerful tools you can use to let your child know that you really like her behavior. Here's an idea that two parents, or a parent and another adult, can use to make a child feel appreciated and noticed.

First, one parent praises the child for behaving:

> "You were very helpful with your brother today. I appreciate how you shared your crayons. I want to make sure that Mom hears about this when she gets home."

Next, this parent praises the child in front of the other parent:

> "Derek played so nicely with his brother today. While I was preparing dinner, they both colored pictures with Derek's new crayons."

Finally, the other parent praises the child:

> "I'm very proud of you, Derek. Dad told me that you played very nicely with your brother today. That's really helped Dad out. Thanks."

If you are a single parent, you can use a grandparent, neighbor or family friend as your partner in giving Super Praise. Any adult whose approval your child will value can fill the role of the second person offering praise.

Behavior Motivators

Your praise is your most powerful motivator. But from time to time it's fun to show your appreciation and encourage positive behavior with a little something extra.

Marbles in a Jar

Reward your child's good behavior choices with this motivational activity. Get a small glass jar and some marbles. Every time you catch your child being good, praise your child's behavior and then drop a marble into the jar. Explain that when there are twenty (or any number of) marbles in the jar, you will reward her excellent behavior with a special privilege.

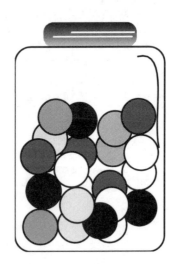

Behavior Charts

Draw a simple chart on a sheet of construction paper (or use the ones at the back of this book). Each day that your child follows the specific behavior that you are working on (keeping room tidy, doing homework, speaking respectfully to others), put a check in one of the boxes on the chart. When a specific number of checks have been accumulated, your child receives something special from you. Place the chart in a prominent place (refrigerator door, bulletin board) as a positive reminder of the benefits of good behavior choices.

**Stay On Target
With Good Behavior**

Make a check for each day you _____
BEHAVIOR YOU ARE WORKING ON

Encourage good behavior with special rewards and privileges.

Here are just a few special ways to encourage your child to make good behavior choices. Just remember, follow-through is as important with rewards as it is with consequences. If you promise your child a special reward for her good behavior choices, give it when it has been earned.

- Rent a video.
- Have a picnic.
- Visit friends.
- Go on a camping trip.
- Visit the library.
- Walk to the park.
- Play a board game with the family.
- Have a friend spend the night.
- Do an arts and crafts project.
- Go rollerblading or bicycle riding.

The positive support you give your child every day is pivotal in helping your child stay on track. Your praise, your words of encouragement, and your gentle guidance and support are what will shape your child into the caring, self-reliant adult she will become.

A hug, a kiss, a smile, a wink, a pat on the shoulder—all of these special, silent signals let your child know how much you appreciate her. Send your child these messages of love and encouragement every single day. Your child never outgrows her need for your love and assurance.

Parents Want to Know
Questions & Answers

Many parents have concerns about implementing a discipline program with their children. By reading through their questions, you may find answers to similar problems you are facing with your child.

Q I'm a single parent. How do I find the time or energy to be as consistent as you say is necessary?

ANSWER: Being a single parent does make the job of disciplining your children much more difficult. But you still can be consistent and effective. Stop believing that just because you are a single parent you cannot get your children to behave. In fact, you will expend far more energy arguing with your children and trying to make them behave if you don't discipline them consistently.

Q We really believe in praising our child for everything he does right, but lately, the more we praise him, the more he acts up. What are we doing wrong?

ANSWER: Too much of a good thing can be as ineffective as not enough. If you go around the house complimenting everything your child does, after a while your praise will lose all its meaning for your son. When you are using praise to motivate good behavior, make it specific and give it immediately. As your child progresses, praise less frequently but keep up other positive attention—smiles, hugs and listening attentively to him. The unconditional love you give your child is crucial in shaping his behavior and self-esteem.

Q I have found time out to be very successful for my four-year-old twins. The only problem is that I forget to monitor how long they have been in time out. Do you have any suggestions?

ANSWER: Invest in a portable kitchen timer. Set the timer for four minutes (a minute for every year of age) and explain that when the timer rings, time out is over.

Q My parents were not big on praising me when I was good and I grew up okay. Why do I need to be different with my kids?

ANSWER: Experience has taught us that the more positive you are with your children, the easier it will be to get them to behave. Your parents may not have needed to use reinforcement with you and your siblings, but times are different. If you choose not to positively reinforce your children's good behavior choices, be aware that you are choosing to offer less motivation for your children to behave.

Another important reason to positively recognize your children's efforts is the direct relationship between parental reactions and self-esteem. A child's self-esteem is built on the positive support received from the significant people in his or her life—and you are the most significant person in your children's lives. Your words of encouragement and your nurturing attitude will greatly increase your children's chances of growing up to be happy, successful adults.

Q I am the only one at home who deals with the kids when they misbehave. My husband is oblivious to the way they carry on. When I discipline them, my husband will not support me. He just says, "Kids will be kids." I can't handle them by myself. Help!

ANSWER: In a two-parent home, one parent can rarely get the children to behave without the active support of his or her spouse. Set aside a specific time when you and your spouse can sit down undisturbed and discuss your concerns at length.

You need to tell your husband in an assertive, direct manner that you need his help. Say, "I need more cooperation from you in dealing with the children. It is in our children's best interests that they know we are a team and that we will both deal with them when they do or do not behave." Once you have laid the groundwork, explain the consequences that will occur if your spouse does not offer you the support you need. "Unless you back me up getting the children to behave, I think they will never learn to behave appropriately." If your husband becomes hostile, evasive or defensive, it may be useful to use the broken-record technique (see page 20) to help you make your point and stick to it and to keep your husband from getting sidetracked. Once he knows that you mean business, involve your husband in planning your discipline efforts. It may be helpful to have him read and discuss the steps in this book.

Q My children don't feel they have to abide by the rules when they have a babysitter. They stay up late, leave their toys scattered around and talk disrespectfully to her. It's getting hard to find a sitter to watch them. What can we do?

ANSWER: Before the babysitter arrives, sit down with your children and discuss the rules for the evening. In a firm, assertive manner state that you expect them to behave appropriately when the babysitter is there: speak respectfully, put toys away after using them, go to bed at a specific time. It is very important to explain what will happen if they choose not to follow these rules (no TV, trip to park, video games). Also explain how you will reward their good behavior if they choose to follow the rules (special family time together, rent a video).

When the babysitter arrives, explain the rules to her, too. Ask her to report any misbehavior at the end of the evening. If problems did arise, make sure to follow through with your consequences the next day. Most importantly, remember to reward your children with praise and a special privilege for behaving well. Your consistent follow-through will ensure success when your children have babysitters in the future.

In Conclusion

It has been our goal in this book to provide you with parenting techniques that can help you encourage appropriate behavior in your child. At the outset of this program, your child may seem upset with this new method of discipline, but don't give in at the first sign of dissension. You love your child and only want to help him grow up in the most caring way possible. It may be a rocky road at first, but in time (probably a shorter time than you might expect), your child will respond. And if you are consistent with your positive encouragement and consequences for misbehavior, your child's behavior will improve.

In parting, keep these points in mind:

- Discipline is a way of growth.

- Children need to be taught how to behave.

- To feel secure, your children need you to set limits.

- Discipline your children with kindness and love.

- Be a positive role model.

Stay On Target
With Good Behavior

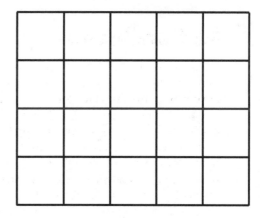

Make a check for each day you _____

BEHAVIOR YOU ARE WORKING ON

All-Star Behavior Chart

Color a star for each day you _____

BEHAVIOR YOU ARE WORKING ON

Out of This World Behavior Chart

Color a planet or star for each day of responsible behavior.

Good Behavior Chart

Color a heart for each day of responsible behavior.